Gearhead Garage

SUPERCARS

PETER BODENSTEINER

BLACK
RABBIT
BOOKS

Bolt is published by Black Rabbit Books
P.O. Box 3263, Mankato, Minnesota, 56002.
www.blackrabbitbooks.com
Copyright © 2017 Black Rabbit Books

Design and Production by Michael Sellner
Photo Research by Rhonda Milbrett

Library of Congress Control Number: 2015954674

HC ISBN: 978-1-68072-036-5   PB ISBN: 978-1-68072-263-5

Printed in the United States at CG Book Printers,
North Mankato, Minnesota, 56003. PO #1790 4/16

CONTENTS

CHAPTER 1

A Spaceship on Wheels

The car cruises by. It looks almost like a rolling spaceship. Its **angles** and curves say that this is no ordinary car. Then its low rumble becomes a roar. The car races off, faster than any other car on the street. But it's not going nearly as fast as it could.

Hard to Define

Supercars are the most **unique** cars in the world. They all have different **features**. To determine if a car is a supercar, it must meet some rules.

Rule #1
It must be
VERY FAST.

Rule #2

It must have an
EYE-CATCHING DESIGN.

It must be
EXPENSIVE.

Rule #3

7

PARTS OF A SUPERCAR

GULLWING DOOR

ENGINE

HEADLIGHTS

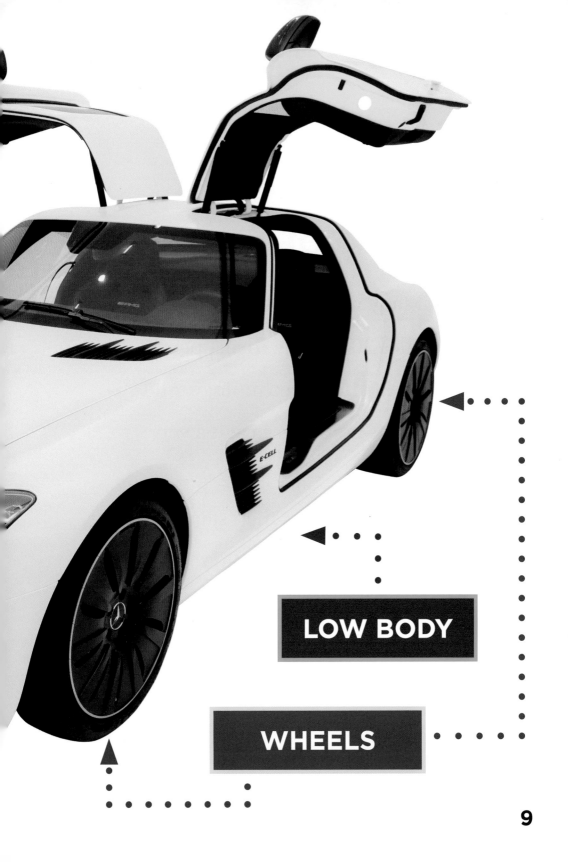

LOW BODY

WHEELS

CHAPTER 2

The History of Supercars

Many people call the 1954 Mercedes 300 SL the first supercar. It used **advanced** technology. And its odd lift-up doors gave it a very different look.

Italian carmakers then started making supercars. The 1966 Lamborghini Miura set the pattern for supercars to come. It had 350 **horsepower**. Its body was low and wide.

MERCEDES
300 SL

PORSCHE 959

Getting Faster

Two supercars became very popular in the 1980s. People loved the Ferrari 288 GTO and Porsche 959. These cars were some of the fastest at the time. Today, both cars are very **valuable**.

Even Faster

In the 1990s, many other companies started building supercars. Each company wanted to build the fastest, coolest cars. The speeds got faster. The prices got higher. And supercars became more popular than ever.

COMPARING *TOP SPEEDS*

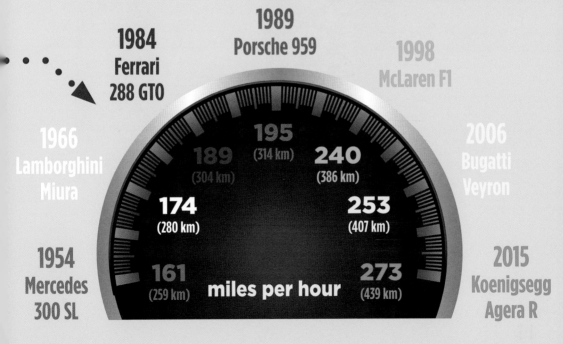

1984
Ferrari
288 GTO

1989
Porsche 959

1998
McLaren F1

1966
Lamborghini
Miura

195
(314 km)

189
(304 km)

240
(386 km)

2006
Bugatti
Veyron

174
(280 km)

253
(407 km)

1954
Mercedes
300 SL

161
(259 km)

miles per hour

273
(439 km)

2015
Koenigsegg
Agera R

AUTOMAKERS THAT BUILD SUPERCARS

From GREAT BRITAIN
Aston Martin
Jaguar
McLaren
From FRANCE
Bugatti

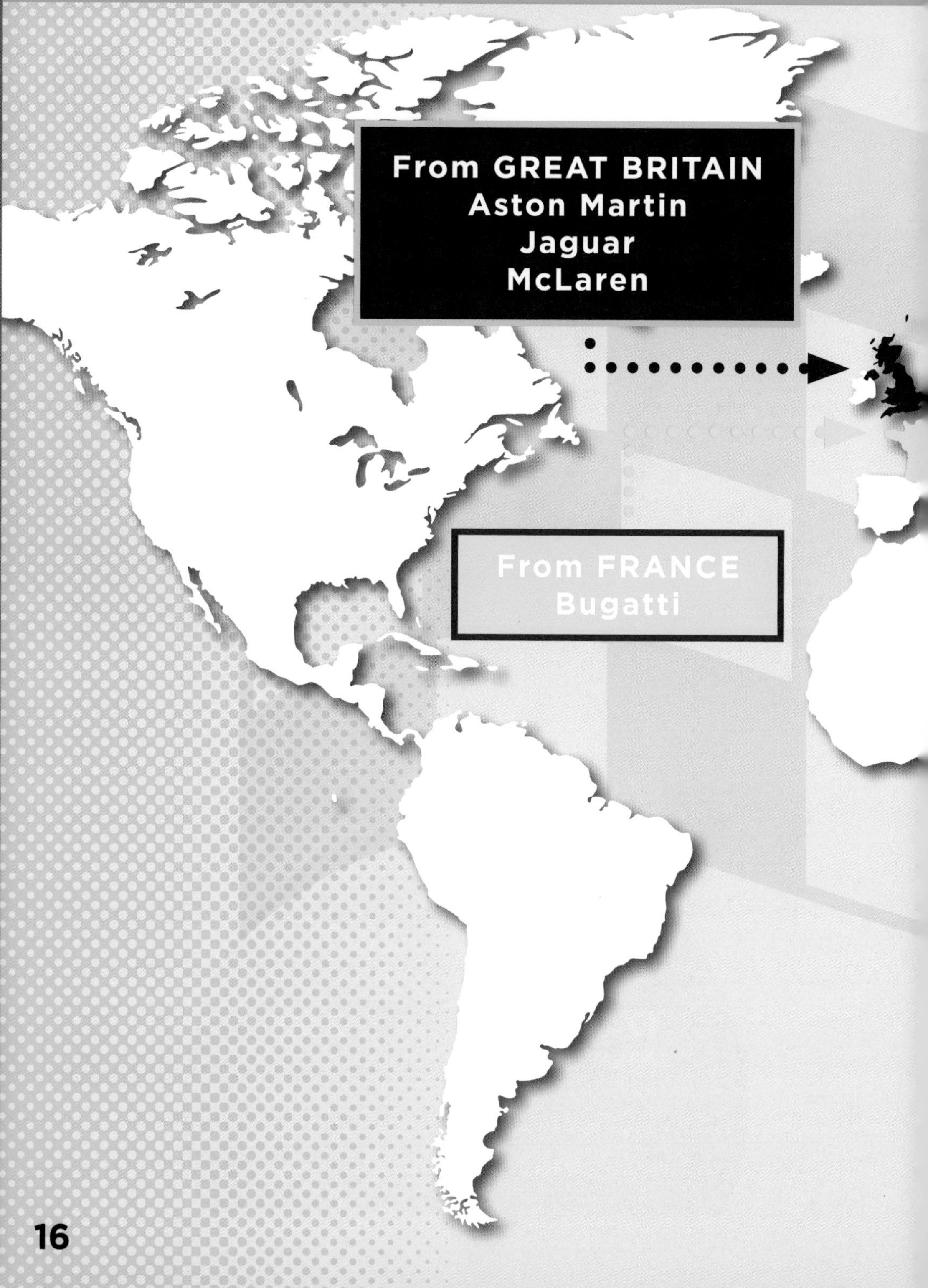

From SWEDEN
Koenigsegg

From GERMANY
Audi
Mercedes-Benz
Porsche

From ITALY
Ferrari
Lamborghini
Maserati
Pagani

CHAPTER 3

High-Tech and High Speed

Many supercars are known for unique doors. "Scissor" doors slide up. They open toward the cars' fronts. Other supercars have doors that open like wings. These are called gullwing doors.

650S

SCISSOR DOORS

By the Numbers

273 MILES (439 KILOMETERS) **PER HOUR**

TOP SPEED OF MODERN SUPERCARS

2.7 SECONDS

TIME FOR THE KOENIGSEGG AGERA R TO GO FROM

0 to 60 MILES

(97 KM) PER HOUR

1

NUMBER OF
ASTON MARTIN BULLDOGS
EVER MADE

$4.8 MILLION
PRICE FOR THE MOST EXPENSIVE SUPERCAR IN 2015

CATERHAM

R500 CC

7

ABOUT 1,000 POUNDS (454 kilograms)

WEIGHT OF THE
SUPERLIGHT
CATERHAM R500

COMPARING HORSEPOWER

1954 Mercedes 300 SL

1984 Ferrari 288 GTO

1992 Bugatti EB 110 Super Sport

2016 Audi R8

time to get from 0 to 60 miles (97 km) per hour

Engines

Supercars must have powerful engines. Some engines can have more than 1,000 horsepower.

Racers in the 1960s began putting engines behind the drivers. This placement made cars faster. Supercars today often have engines in the back.

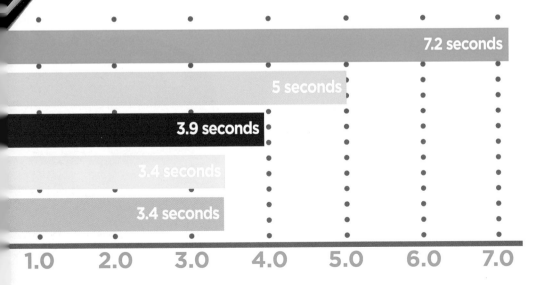

7.2 seconds

5 seconds

3.9 seconds

3.4 seconds

3.4 seconds

1.0   2.0   3.0   4.0   5.0   6.0   7.0

CHAPTER 4

The  of Supercars

Carmakers look for ways to make supercars faster and cooler. Some cars use both gas and electric **motors**. In the future, these motors could make better cars. Some people call these "hypercars."

Plug car in to **charge battery.**

Hypercar uses **battery power** to drive wheels.

Quick and Fun

Some people think future supercars will be all electric. But no matter what changes, some things will stay the same. Supercars will always be quick and

fun to drive.

1954

The first supercar, Mercedes 300 SL, is released.

1966

Lamborghini Miura is released.

1984

Ferrari 288 GTO is released.

1945

World War II ends.

1945

The first people walk on the moon.

1969

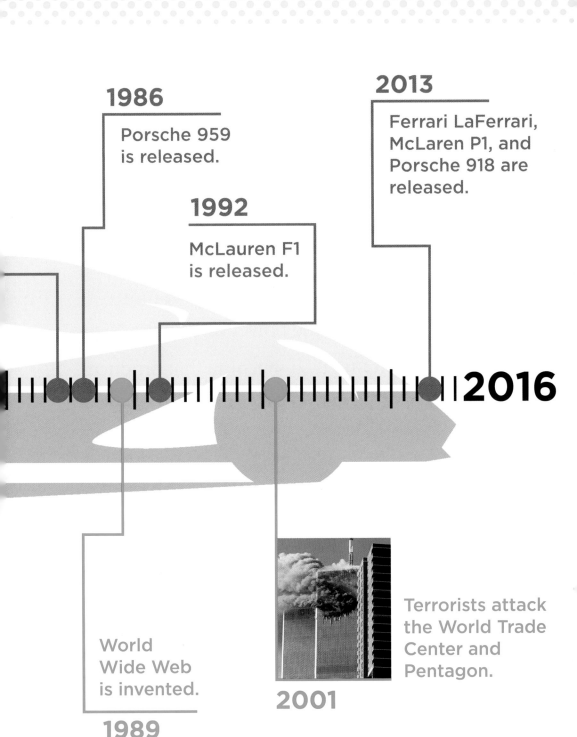

1986

Porsche 959 is released.

1992

McLauren F1 is released.

2013

Ferrari LaFerrari, McLaren P1, and Porsche 918 are released.

2016

World Wide Web is invented.

1989

Terrorists attack the World Trade Center and Pentagon.

2001

advanced (ad-VANSD)—being beyond others in progress

angle (AYN-gul)—the space or shape formed when two lines or surfaces meet

feature (FEE-chur)—an interesting or important part or quality

horsepower (HORS-pow-uhr)—a unit used to measure the power of engines

motor (MO-tur)—a machine that produces motion or power; in cars, it's another word for engine.

unique (yoo-NEEK)—very special or unusual

valuable (VAL-yoo-bul)—worth a lot of money

BOOKS

Cruz, Calvin. *McLaren 12C.* Car Crazy. Minneapolis: Bellwether Media, Inc., 2016.

Gifford, Clive. *Car Crazy.* New York: DK Publishing, 2012.

Turner, Tracey. *Supercars.* Head-to-Head. Mankato, MN: Smart Apple Media, 2016.

WEBSITES

List of All the Supercars
www.supercarworld.com/cgi-bin/listall.cgi

Supercars
www.topgear.com/car-news/supercars

The Supercar Story
www.smithsonianchannel.com/shows/the-supercar-story/0/130308

INDEX